SEE INSIDE

A CASTLE

SERIES EDITOR **R.J. UNSTEAD**

WARWICK PRESS

Series Editor and Author
R. J. Unstead

Illustrations
Dan Escott   Brian Lewis
Richard Hook

Revised edition published 1986 by Warwick Press,
387 Park Avenue South, New York, New York 10016.
First published in 1986 by Kingfisher Books Limited.
Originally published by Hutchinson & Co. Limited 1977.

Copyright © Grisewood & Dempsey Limited 1977, 1986.
Printed in Hong Kong

A Fortress Home

A castle was the fortress and home of a lord who built it to protect his lands and defend his family and followers from attack. Castles of this kind seem to have appeared first in France during the 11th century. After William the Conqueror had seized England, he gave permission to his leading nobles to erect castles in order to keep the defeated Saxons in check. They had to work quickly, and here you can see one of the motte-and-bailey castles which, with forced labor, they put up in a matter of a week or two. It consists of a wooden tower on an earth mound connected to a bailey or courtyard. Sited at a crossroads, by a river, inside or near a town, it dominates the countryside and serves as a base from which the Norman lord can rule the district. In case of attack and loss of the bailey, the garrison can retreat to the tower and hold out there until a relieving force arrives. Wooden buildings and fences can obviously be smashed or set on fire, so, as soon as possible, the Normans will replace them by stone walls and towers.

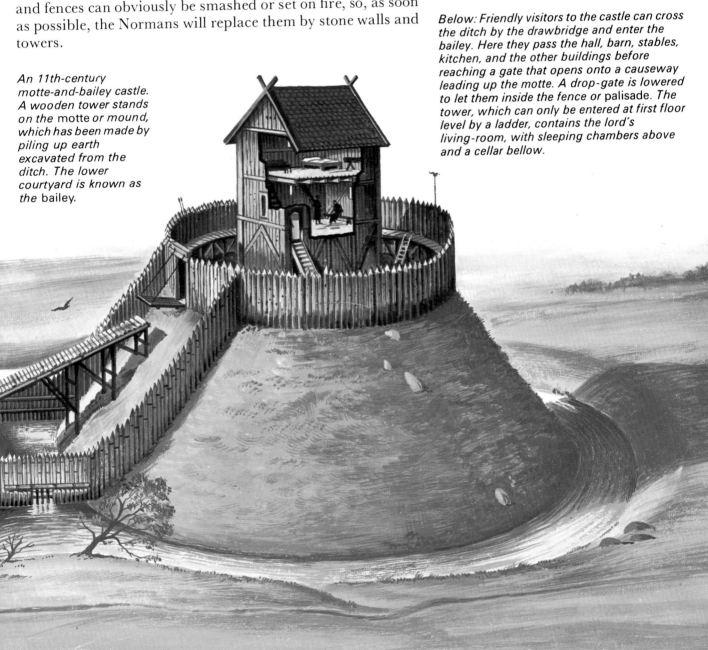

A shell keep, a natural development of the motte-and-bailey castle. A stone wall replaces the wooden palisade on top of the motte. Buildings, such as the hall, chapel and kitchen have been erected inside the shell.

Below: Friendly visitors to the castle can cross the ditch by the drawbridge and enter the bailey. Here they pass the hall, barn, stables, kitchen, and the other buildings before reaching a gate that opens onto a causeway leading up the motte. A drop-gate is lowered to let them inside the fence or palisade. The tower, which can only be entered at first floor level by a ladder, contains the lord's living-room, with sleeping chambers above and a cellar bellow.

An 11th-century motte-and-bailey castle. A wooden tower stands on the motte or mound, which has been made by piling up earth excavated from the ditch. The lower courtyard is known as the bailey.

The Stone Keep

Here is the direct successor of the motte-and-bailey castle – a stone castle whose strongest point is a massive tower known as the *donjon* or *keep*. Because of its great weight, it stands, not on an earth motte, but on flat ground or a natural hill. It has immensely thick walls, with four square corner turrets and small windows which, on lower levels, are no more than slits. For defense, entry is by a staircase to the second floor, the stairs leading up to the *forebuilding* at the side of the great tower. The keep stands in the *inner bailey*, a courtyard in which are placed the kitchen, granary, and other storerooms. This bailey is defended by a curtain wall, strengthened by a gatehouse, moat, and projecting towers. Beyond, stretches the *outer bailey*, a big enclosure containing domestic buildings, stables, a garden, and exercise yard. High thick walls, D-shaped and round towers, gatehouse, drawbridge, and moat complete the defenses.

The spiral staircase winds upward to the right. In wielding his sword, the knight coming up is hampered by the center-post, but the defender is not.

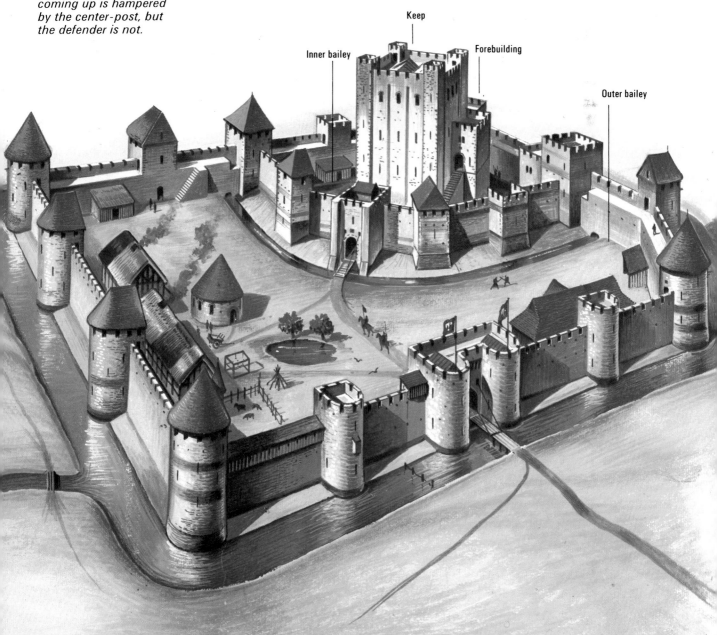

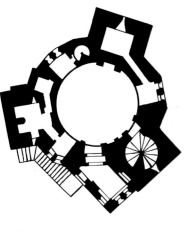

Above: This is a section through the keep of Orford Castle in Suffolk, England, built by Henry II as an improvement on the square keep. It is round on the inside, but the outside is a polygon.

Three large towers, which jut out to protect the walls, contain the spiral staircase and many small rooms, including two kitchens, an unusual feature in a 12th-century keep.

This keep which is divided by a thick cross-wall, has a basement and three stories. Garrison quarters and the well-head are on the second floor. The Great Hall and the lord's solar on the third, sleeping chambers on the fourth, with roof and battlements above. Notice the chapel in the forebuilding.

Right: Here, in the solar, maids are preparing a bath for the lady of the castle. Other members of the household are probably going to share the water, since it is quite common for several persons to bathe together. As soap, they use animal fat mixed with wood ash. One of the lady's damsels sits in the window alcove to obtain light for her embroidery.

Below: Dinner in the Great Hall, where the lord, his lady and their guests sit on the dais, at a long table covered with a white cloth. A page waits upon them. The rest of the household sit lower down on benches at trestle tables which can be taken down when the Hall is needed for games, dancing or meetings. Notice the garde-robe (lavatory) in the side room.

The Great Hall and Solar

The center of all domestic life is the Great Hall, whether it is situated in the keep or in a fine new building in the bailey. Dinner is served here every day, as well as splendid banquets when the king or some great lord or bishop comes to stay. The lord meets his chief officials and tenants in the Hall, issues orders and listens to grievances. It is the meeting-place for the barony court, where wrongdoers are generally punished by fines, which provide a useful source of income for the lord. Social activities take place here, dancing, high jinks from the mummers, music played by the minstrels, storytelling and games, such as chess and "tables," a kind of backgammon played with dice.

The Great Hall is often divided by a thick cross wall, the smaller part containing the solar or withdrawing-room. This may be the lord's bedroom or he may also have a private chamber beyond. At all events, the solar is warmer and less uncomfortable than any other room in the castle. The lord retires here, but he also receives important visitors in the solar, where, owing to the lack of chairs, the bed is used as a seat during daytime.

THE ARMORER

The armorer is an important figure at the castle. While the knights usually provide their own equipment, he has to keep stocks of weapons and armor for the lesser men-at-arms and for the lord's tenants who, when they come in to do their guard duty, invariably arrive poorly equipped. So he keeps a stock of bows, bowstrings, bolts, arrows, helmets, and swords. Mail has to be repaired and kept free from rust by cleaning with sand and vinegar. Swords must be sharpened, helmets mended and the big catapult on the battlement kept in working order and supplied with stones.

Daily work in the Castle

When the lord arrives on one of his visits or the king comes to stay or war threatens, all is bustle and activity at the castle. Supplies of every kind – cattle, sheep, poultry, eggs, flour, fish, fruit and vegetables – have to be brought in from local manors. Cooks, baker, dairy-maids, and butler (who sees to the beer and wine) prepare food and drink for the household. Carpenters and masons repair walls and roofs; smith, farrier, and armorer see to horses, wagons, and weapons; a clerk keeps accounts. Chaplain, laundress and sewing maids carry out their various duties. Messengers scurry to and fro and the sergeant at arms inspects the garrison, while the steward reports progress to his

Above: A busy scene in the kitchen. At the table, a side of beef is being cut up for the pot, a pair of plucked geese will soon be spitted, a cook makes pastry, another receives a bag of spice from the wardrober. Water is being drawn from the well, while a serf carries faggots to the fire, which is being made ready to boil cauldrons of stew and to roast geese on the spit. Notice the bread oven, the barrels in the store and upstairs, the clerk at his accounts.

Above right: In the scullery the scullion is in charge of the plates, dishes and cooking vessels.

lord. In some castles the kitchen is in the stone keep, but in most cases, cooking and various other household activities take place in the wooden buildings erected in the courtyard. In time, they will be replaced by a range of stone buildings.

The task of organizing this household which varies in number from perhaps a dozen persons to two hundred, falls upon the baron, his lady, and the steward.

In peacetime, after a stay of a few weeks, local food supplies have been eaten and the garde-robes (lavatories) and moat are foul, so the household moves on to another castle. The permanent staff then clears up the mess.

In the Walled Enclosure

In this enclosure, starting from the left-hand side, you see the roof of a store shed (1), then the kitchen with its elaborate chimney (2). Next is a store and the brewhouse (3). Then comes the Great Hall (4), with its solar and guest chambers above; thatched barn and stables (5) are built against the wall, next to the piggery (6). The last three buildings are the castle's handsome chapel (7), the smithy (8) where horses are shod and armor and weapons mended, and the wagon shed. The lord's fenced-in-garden contains fruit trees, beehives, his lady's herb beds and a big dovecot whose plump birds provide fresh meat for the top table in winter. In the courtyard outside the fence, a kitchen maid fetches water from the well as hogs root about in the mud near the haystacks. A company of soldiers going out on training exercise passes a returning hunting party.

The solar is the lord's private room and frequently his bedchamber. It is by far the most luxurious room in the castle, containing a four-poster bed, with fine hangings and the family coat-of-arms above. Furnishings include a couple of chests, one for clothes and one for documents, silver plate and gold coins, a stool, a tall stand for candles or a torch, a ewer and basin, tapestry on walls and even a mat on the floor. The hooded fireplace provides warmth in winter and the window, looking toward the courtyard, is big enough to make the solar light and airy.

The wall-walk runs through each tower, enabling the garrison to meet an attack at any point.

Notice the strong doors that can be shut to turn each tower into a miniature keep. Rounded towers and walls withstand battering rams and missiles better than angled ones.

Above: In a corner of the Great Hall, the chaplain is giving a lesson to two pages. Sons of noble parents, they have been sent to the castle to learn manners and knightly behavior. Behind them, the lady of the household gives instruction to one of her sewing-women. Notice the handsome screen with doors leading to the kitchen and buttery; the minstrels play in the gallery above.

Daily Life in the Castle

A castle is a home as well as a fortress. Indeed, a hundred years may pass without its inmates suffering the horrors of a siege. The baron's habit of moving about the country means that the household rarely settles for long in one place but, while in residence at the castle, the lord inspects his lands, sees his chief tenants, imposes justice, enjoys hunting and hawking, and entertains his guests.

A prime task of his officials is to organize food and drink supplies and to see to the cooking and serving. A host of servants carry out all kinds of daily tasks – fuel and water have to be fetched, letters and accounts written, horses groomed and shod, linen washed, clothes made and mended, ale brewed and loaves baked. The priest takes morning service in the chapel and later gives lessons to the pages. Weapon training is held in the outer bailey, while the lady of the castle supervises the upbringing of her children, the making of medicines and ointments, and the giving of alms to the poor.

Below: A lad at archery practice: from boyhood, almost everyone learns to use weapons.

12

THE STEWARD

After the baron and his wife, the most important person in the castle is the steward. A knight and often a relative of the lord, he acts as his deputy, holding courts in the castle, appointing officials such as the bailiffs and reeves, fixing rents and tenancies of farms, supervising the smooth running of everyday life. Above all, he is responsible for every penny of the lord's expenditure and the drawing-up of the daily account.

From time to time, a tournament is held to provide entertainment and military training. Here, in the "joust of peace," two knights charge each other, left side to left side. On the left, a combat between dismounted knights.

SPORTS AND AMUSEMENTS

The best-loved sport is hunting. Everyone hunts hares and rabbits, but deer are reserved for the king and nobles who are granted permission to hunt on their own estates.

Falconry is another aristocratic sport, with peregrines and goshawks trained by expert falconers. From time to time, a tournament is held when mock combats and jousts between mounted knights take place. Young squires practice riding at the "quintain," a target with a weight that swings around and hits the rider, if he is not quick.

Indoors, chess is a favorite game; dice, too, is popular but less highly thought of. A few people own books, but most prefer to pass the evening with story-telling, songs, jokes and dancing. In great households, the company may be entertained by a harper and minstrels; occasionally, jugglers and acrobats are hired to amuse the guests.

Left: A hunting party crosses the drawbridge on its way to the forest. The lord and his guest are accompanied by the falconer, a bowman and the huntsman with two hounds.

The Castle's Defenses

In the days of motte-and-bailey castles and of the square keep, defense was usually passive – the garrison merely held out, hoping that relief would arrive and drive the enemy away. With the building of more advanced castles, defense becomes more active, for the men-at-arms can move rapidly around the wall-walk. Overhanging *hoardings* and *machicolations* enable the defense to assault an enemy battering away at the base of walls or towers. Walls are made extra thick and splayed out to counter the mine and battering-ram; the gateway, always likely to be the main point of attack, is strengthened with portcullis, *murder-holes* and an additional outwork called the barbican (see page 16). The garrison can launch counter-attacks by sallying out from one gateway to take the enemy in the rear while he assaults the main gateway or they may use a small postern gate called a *sally-port*.

Successful defense depends greatly on the spirit and loyalty of the garrison and on a good supply of food, drinking-water, weapons and missiles. The biggest dangers are treachery and starvation.

Above: The embrasure or splayed opening on the inner side of a loophole provides a safe place from which an archer can fire at the enemy. He normally uses a crossbow and is accompanied by a lad or varlet who loads a second bow for him, so that he can keep up a rapid rate of fire.

Left to right, a plain vertical loophole; then one with a fishtail base; next, a cruciform loophole whose base may be sloped downward to help the archer aim at the ground. The round holes at the end of the loophole's arms are called oilettes *and the last example shows a loophole with a gun-port below for a handgun.*

HOARDINGS AND MACHICOLATIONS

To enable the defenders to drop missiles on enemies at the base of walls, wooden galleries or *hoardings* are pushed out from the battlements. They rest on beams passed through *put-log* holes at wall-walk level (right). The hoardings, which are usually erected as soon as warfare threatens, can be destroyed by fire or catapulted boulders. So, in some castles, they are replaced by permanent parapets (left) resting on stone brackets called *corbels*. The space between each pair of corbels is called a *machicolation*.

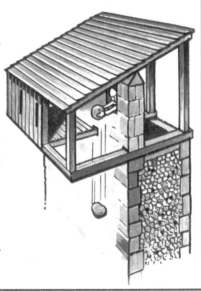

Gatehouse and Barbican

Since the entrance to a castle is its most vulnerable point, it has been strengthened until it has become a keep-gatehouse. Two massive machicolated towers guard the entrance passage, which is further defended by a drawbridge, a pair of iron-studded doors and two portcullises. If enemies do enter the passage they are assailed from loopholes on either side and through *murder-holes* set in the ceiling. You can see these arrangements in the picture, as well as a hall and living rooms. The constable or commander of the castle now lives in the gatehouse with his personal followers, for he may not fully trust the mercenaries who make up the rest of the garrison. The gatehouse is so strong that he can hold out after the rest of the castle has been captured.

As an additional defense, an outwork called the *barbican* has been built on the far side of the moat. It possesses all the traditional defenses and an enemy who overcomes them, will still have to cross an open causeway exposed to fire from the main gateway, towers, and walls.

Above: Here are two types of drawbridge. The first one is a seesaw type, pivoted on an axle, so that a heavy weight on the inner end causes the bridge to swing upright, barring the entrance. In the lower picture, the hinged bridge is attached by chains to a beam above that pulls it up quickly.

Left: This iron-studded double-door opens inward, but cannot easily be forced because of the draw-bars which run in and out of deep slots cut in the wall.

In the main drawing on the right, a friendly visitor arrives at the barbican. The drawbridge is lowered to admit him and he will pass over the causeway and through numerous defenses (notice the gun-ports) to enter the gatehouse. In addition to the fortifications, he will find it contains living quarters, sleeping-chambers and a solar whose chimney leads up to the wall-walk. At the top, there is a room with a kitchen where meals are prepared for the guards who man the battlements.

gun-ports

Murder-holes

causeway

DAN E

The Perfect Castle

A most important development in castle design – the *concentric* castle, which means having a common center – occurs in the late 13th and early 14th centuries. Its essential feature is an outer and lower ring of defenses. There is no keep, no final refuge or strongpoint and no weak spot, for every part of the defense protects or is protected by another part. If the attackers *do* break down or scale the outer wall, they will not find an inch of cover in the bailey. The defenders, having withdrawn to the inner defenses, can concentrate their fire at any danger point.

It is said that the knights of western Europe learned about concentric defenses while on crusade in the Near East. In Britain, Henry III added outer defenses to Dover Castle and the Tower of London to turn them into concentric castles, and his son, Edward I, built some magnificent examples in Wales.

Above: Here you can see how the defenders on the inner fortifications can fire over the heads of those manning the outer walls and towers.

This plan of Beaumaris Castle in Wales reveals a remarkable symmetry or balance. A keep-gatehouse on one side is matched by a keep-gatehouse on the other. Round towers stand at the four corners and midway on each flank. Each tower on the outer wall is matched by its fellow on the opposite side.

Right: Krak des Chevaliers, Syria — a fine example of a concentric castle.

Below: This is how Beaumaris Castle would have looked if Edward I had completed it. Four lofty round towers and two D-shaped towers protect the inner bailey, with two huge gatehouses. These massive defenses overlook the low outer wall with its towers and small gateway protected by a barbican. A defended pier guards the dock for ships coming up the river.

The Castle under Attack

The attackers' first move was to completely surround the castle to prevent the entry of any stores, in the hope of starving the garrison into surrender. The next step was to discharge an assortment of missiles at the walls and over the battlements. Siege machines hurled heavy stones, outsize arrows, rotting animal carcasses, even the bodies of captured enemies, and the deadly Greek fire. This was a flammable liquid, based on naphtha, that was used to inspire terror and to set fire to domestic buildings, storerooms, and wooden hoardings.

Meanwhile, under cover of this barrage and of showers of arrows, gangs of men moved up to fill in a portion of the moat in order to make use of the *belfry*. This was a tower on wheels, from whose top archers could rake the battlements, while a bridge was let down on to the wall so that attackers could enter the castle itself. Others would also use scaling ladders to storm the walls, while some might be assaulting the main gate with battering ram. The aim was to engage the defenders as fully as possible in hope of breaking into the castle at one point or another. If these efforts failed, the attackers would fall back on slower methods – such as mining and starvation.

FIRE POWER

An early cannon: guns of this type were in use from the middle of the 14th century. This is a muzzle-loader, a cylinder made of iron strips held in place by hoops of iron and laid on the ground in a frame with a strong backing to take the kick of the explosion. The gunpowder is put in first, then the ball. The powder is then fired through a touch-hole bored in the top of the barrel.

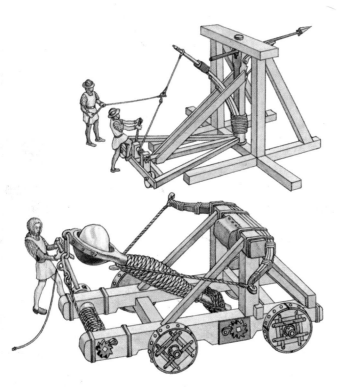

Below: Two types of catapult. The one below fires a heavy bolt, often tipped with some flammable material. The bottom picture shows a giant crossbow, the beam of which is winched back to propel a large stone with terrific force.

Below is a trebuchet *whose great arm is being winched down; when released, the counter-weight makes it fly upright to hurl its missile over the walls.*

A siege in progress: Siege-engines and cannon have inflicted some damage on the castle; archers fire from behind movable screens called mantlets and, by means of scaling ladders and a belfry, the attackers have reached the wall-walk.

Building a Castle

In the picture opposite, a tower is nearing completion, for the wall-walk is partly finished, the parapet has been started and timber framing is being hoisted for the roof, which will be finally covered with slates, shingles or perhaps lead.

Construction is being carried out by a large work force – 868 men were employed at Harlech, about 1,500 at Conway Castle and, at Beaumaris, 400 skilled masons have been taken on, 30 smiths and carpenters, 200 carters, and 1,000 other workers such as ditchers, hewers, stone-breakers, levelers and well-diggers. The men use spades, pickaxes, hammers, and baskets for carrying earth and stones, for the only mechanical aids are simple hoists fitted with pulley and tackle. You can see that the core of the walls is not made of solid stone, but of flints and rubble; mixed with mortar and strengthened with heavy chains, the mass will set as hard as rock. Arches, doorways and most of the outer surfaces are made of smooth hewn stone call *ashlar*.

Directing the whole operation is an architect or master mason, one of that elite class of experts who can command high salaries. A master mason has to be able to read and write, to understand the "mysteries" of geometry and to have had first-hand experience of every aspect of the mason's craft. Like his chief assistants, the carpenters and masons, he has come a long way, possibly from overseas, to work on a project that offers high wages, but the unskilled laborers are local men pressed into service by the lord's baliff.

When King Edward I decided to have his Welsh castles built by the finest architect in Christendom, he invited Master James of St. George (who took his name from a place near Lyons belonging to the Count of Savoy, for whom he worked) to come to England and enter the royal service. As Master of the King's Works, James receives the handsome salary of 3 shillings a day with a pension of half that amount for his wife if she survives him.

The King has been so pleased with his architect's skill in designing each of the great castles differently – Rhuddlan, Flint, Conway, Caernarvon, Harlech, and Beaumaris – organizing the transport of vast quantities of building materials and directing the entire operation involving a small army of workers, that he has made him Constable of Harlech Castle. Master James has also served the King in Scotland, notably in connection with Linlithgow Castle, and has been rewarded with the grant of the Flintshire manor of Mostyn.

Styles of masonry varied greatly from castle to castle. These different styles provide important clues for dating castles and understanding the influences behind their construction. Small square stones were used for the earliest castles. Later, these were replaced with large rectangular blocks. In the eleventh century stones were often laid diagonally in a herringbone pattern. Leaving the surface of the stone uncut, (*en bosse*), became a popular decorative device on castles built in Germany and the Middle East. But on the whole, intricate design and delicate architectural features were not of primary importance to the exterior of a castle. Built for defense, they depended greatly on their mass and solidity.

Here is a delightful carving in Salisbury Cathedral, England, showing a castle in course of construction. Laborers carry the stones to the masons.

SOME FAMOUS CASTLES

Left: In 1472 the people of Volterra, Italy, rebelled against Florentine rule. To quell the uprising, Lorenzo de'Medici built the fortress of Volterra.

Right: The castle of Hohensalzburg, Austria, was traditionally the castle of the archbishop. Begun in 1077, it was added onto until the 17th century. In the late Middle Ages parts of the interior were beautifully decorated with red marble columns and paneled ceilings. The castle underwent its only siege during the Peasant's Revolt of 1525.

Carcassone, France (left) and Bodiam Castle, England (above) are fine examples of medieval fortresses.

In Britain, there are scores of castles that can be visited. Among the most interesting are the Tower of London, Dover, Warwick, Ludlow, Caernarvon, Conway, Harlech, Framlingham, Orford, Goodrich, Bodiam, Caerphilly, Portchester, Tantallon, Kildrummie, Borthwick, Claypotts. Famous castles in Europe include Carcassonne, Aigues-Mortes and Falaise in France; Chillon, Switzerland, Almeria and Almodovar, Spain; Hohensalzburg, Austria; Ghent, Belgium; Volterra and Castel del Monte, Italy; Schönburg, Germany, and Almourol, Portugal. The best-known Crusader castles are Krak des Chevaliers and Sahyun in Syria.

Right: This painting of peasants working the land outside the castle of Lusignan in western France is from "The Book of Hours," made for the Duke of Berry, brother of the King of France, in 1400.

Overleaf: Knights jousting – an illustration from a 14th century history written by the French chronicler Jean Froissart. Jousts were friendly but dangerous mock battles which were performed before hundreds of spectators.

CRUSADER CASTLES

At the time of the First Crusade, castles in Europe were little more than a tower on a mound, surrounded by a palisade and a ditch. Hence, the Crusaders were vastly impressed when they saw the sophisticated defenses of cities like Constantinople, Nicaea, and Antioch, as well as the strongholds built by Byzantines and Arabs throughout these ancient lands.

The Crusaders learned much from what they saw. But, in order to defend their hard-won gains, they had to build somewhat differently from the enemy. Always short of manpower, they had to make their castles exceptionally strong and difficult to approach by selecting sites on cliffs, hill-tops and rocky crags.

Furthermore, the castle had to serve as the residence of the lord, his family and retainers, as well as the headquarters from which he ruled his feudal estate, sometimes a whole province. The *enceinte*, or walled enclosure, had to be big enough to shelter local inhabitants, flocks and herds during enemy raids.

Early Crusader castles, like Ibelin, Beth Gibelet and Blanche-garde, near Jerusalem, were built on a quadrilateral plan, with four towers and a keep. Belvoir, similar but much larger and with ditches cut deep into the rock, overlooked the valley of the River Jordan. Marqab (or Margat), a fortress more than $1\frac{1}{2}$ miles ($2\frac{1}{2}$ kilometers) in circumference, stood on the summit of a mountain spur from which the Knights Hospitallers controlled the route from Antioch. They rebuilt their other great stronghold, Krak des Chevaliers, on the border of Tripoli, as the perfect concentric castle, with three lines of defense – moat, outer walls, higher inner walls, dominated by towers, rounded, square and projecting.

Almost impregnable, Krak defied twelve sieges and only fell in 1271 because it had but a tenth of the garrison it needed.

The other great military order, the Knights Templars, favored a single *enceinte* for their castles at Tortosa and Athlit; the German castle, Montfort, also had a single *enceinte*. On the other hand, Sahyun (Saone), a Byzantine fort on a narrow rocky ledge, was converted into an immensely strong castle with ditches and three lines of walls and towers. Yet it fell to Saladin in three days, a disaster which illustrates the Crusaders' fatal weakness. Lack of manpower made it impossible to maintain effective defense or to send relief forces, causing garrisons to lose heart and accept defeat.

However, the military importance of the Crusader castles was that returning knights brought back to Europe ideas which influenced castle-building right up until the introduction of gunfire.

Above: The castle of Montfort in Israel became the possession of the Teutonic Knights during the Sixth Crusade.

Left: Sir Roger de Trumpington (note the trumpet on his shield) who probably fought in the last Crusade led by Louis IX of France and Prince Edward (later Edward I) of England. Edward reached Acre, too late to save Krak des Chevaliers which fell in 1271. Sir Roger's brass, the second oldest in Great Britain, is dated 1289.

IMPORTANT HAPPENINGS

	Europe	Middle East	
413		**413–1150** Eastern Emperors built Constantinople's colossal defenses.	**413**

<table>
<tr><td rowspan="2" valign="top">

1150

</td>
<td valign="top">

*c*950 Motte-and bailey fortifications in use in Normandy. Earliest known castle built at Doue-la-Fontaine, France.

*c*1050 Edward the Confessor invites Normans to build a castle near Ludlow, on Welsh border.

1066 Dover Castle founded by King Harold; enlarged by William I who has Tower of London built in southeast corner of Roman wall.

1068–1100 Norman Conquest consolidated by castles at Warwick, Windsor, York, Richmond, Peveril, Rochester, and Colchester.

1086–1200 Era of stone donjon or keep as the castle strongpoint.

1100–1200 Moorish castles in Spain. Motte-and-bailey castles erected along Welsh border, in Ireland and Scotland.

1150–1250 Holy Roman Emperors erect castles all over Germany; Frederick II of Hohenstauffen also builds in Italy.

1154–1189 Henry II builds and modernizes many castles; curtain walls begin to supersede the keep.

1196 Chateau Gaillard ("Saucy Castle") built by Richard I in Normandy; captured by Philip Augustus in 1204.

</td>
<td valign="top">

*c*998 Byzantine engineers fortify Antioch on a scale which astounds the Crusaders 100 years later.

1095 Pope Urban II preaches the crusade to the Franks.

1096–1099 First Crusade reaches Constantinople, captures Antioch and Jerusalem.

1100–1120 Four Crusader states established: known as Outremer. Crusaders capture towns, build castles and rule as feudal overlords.

1115 Baldwin I, King of Jerusalem, builds castle of Montreal, south of Dead Sea.

*c*1140 King Fulk builds three great castles – Ibelin, Blanchegarde, and Beth Gibelin – to protect Jerusalem.

1142 Kerak of Moab Castle built to dominate route of attackers from Egypt. Krak des Chevaliers ceded to the Hospitallers.

1144 Crusader kingdom of Edessa lost.

1147–1149 Second Crusade (Louis VII of France and Conrad III of Germany) ends in total failure.

1187 Jerusalem is captured by Saladin.

1189–1192 Third Crusade led by Philip II of France, Frederick Barbarossa, Richard Coeur-de-Lion, fails to recapture Jerusalem.

</td>
<td rowspan="2" valign="top">

1150

</td></tr>
<tr>
<td valign="top">

1275–1325 Edward I's "masterpieces of fortification" in N. Wales (Flint, Rhuddlan, Conway, Caernarvon, Harlech, Beaumaris) included walled enclosures, gatehouses, concentric defenses.

1300–1350 "Tower-house" castles play important role in Scottish Wars of Independence.

1327 Capture of Caerphilly Castle, largest, strongest castle ever erected in Britain.

1346 (onward) Cannons begin to be used in battle; gunports are inserted into castle walls. Brick castles built at Hurstmonceux, Tattershall, Caister and in Holland to no avail.

1538–1543 Henry VIII's coastal castles are really artillery forts with medieval features such as the moat, drawbridge, and portcullis.

1600–1700 Wars in England, France, Germany and the Low Countries show that gunfire has made castles obsolete. Where they survive, as in Scotland, France and Germany, they do so as the picturesque residences of wealthy aristocrats.

</td>
<td valign="top">

shamefully sacked by French and Flemish Crusaders.

*c*1205 Krak des Chevaliers rebuilt by Hospitallers as the perfect concentric castle.

1229 Sixth Crusade: Emperor Frederick II ("Stupor Mundi") regains Jerusalem by guile and is crowned King.

1248–1254 Seventh Crusade to Egypt led by Louis IX ("Saint Louis") of France.

1271 Krak, too thinly garrisoned, is captured by Sultan Baibars.

1285 Muslims capture Marqab (or Margat) Castle by mining.

1291 Surrender of Acre to Sultan al-Ashraf marks the effective end of the Crusades.

</td></tr>
</table>

| **1600** | | | **1600** |

GLOSSARY OF TERMS

Allure A wall-walk.

Ashlar Squared blocks of smooth stone.

Aventail Protection for the face, made of mail.

Bailey Ward or courtyard inside the walls of a castle.

Barbican Outer defense of a main gateway.

Bartizan An overhanging corner turret.

Bastion A corner tower, open at the rear.

Belfry A wooden siege-tower.

Belvedere A raised turret or pavilion.

Berm Space between castle wall and moat.

Buttress A pillar strengthening a wall.

Chevron molding Molding in form of inverted V's a favorite Norman decoration.

Corbel A stone bracket.

Crenellations Battlements at top of a tower or wall.

Curtain Stone wall surrounding the bailey; also any castle wall.

Donjon Great tower or keep.

Drawbridge Wooden bridge spanning a pit or moat which could be raised toward the gatehouse.

Drum Tower Round tower built into a wall.

Embrasure Window opening, open space in battlements.

En bosse The surface of stone that is left uncut, also called rusticated masonry.

Enceinte The enclosure or fortified area of a castle.

Forebuilding A structure against keep protecting the stairway and entrance.

Gambeson A quilted piece of clothing meant to be worn under armor.

Garde Robe Lavatory, latrine.

Glacis A bank sloping down from a fort or castle which acts as a defense against invaders.

Great helm An iron helmet that completely covers the head.

Gun-loop Opening for a gun.

Hauberk A coat or shirt of mail.

Hoarding Wooden gallery from which missiles could be dropped.

Keep Great tower.

Loophole Slit for light, air or shooting through.

Machicolations Holes in a stone parapet.

Mangonel Stone-throwing machine.

Merlon Solid part of battlement.

Mantlet A movable wooden shield.

Meurtriere "Murder hole," an opening in roof of a passage.

Motte A mound of earth.

Oilette Round opening at base of a loophole.

Oubliette A dungeon reached by a trap door.

Pele or Peel A small tower for defense purposes, found in Scotland.

Penthouse Roofed shed on wheels for protection of men working a battering-ram.

Portcullis Grating lowered to protect a doorway.

Postern A back gate or small gateway.

Put-logs Beams placed in holes to support a hoarding.

Revet To face a surface with stone slabs for added strength.

Shell-keep Stone wall around the top of a motte.

Saracen Another word for Arab Muslims in Crusader times.

Slight To deliberately damage a castle to make it unfit for use.

Solar Lord's private room.

Trebuchet A giant sling.

INDEX

PHOTOGRAPHIC ACKNOWLEDGEMENTS
The publishers wish to thank the following for supplying photographs for this book: Page 19 Robert Harding; 23 Sonia Halliday; 24 Italian State Tourist Office *top,* Hubmann, Salzburg *bottom*; 25 Zefa *left*; Robert Harding *top right*; Giraudon, Paris *bottom*; 26–27 British Museum; 28 Ronald Sheridan *center*, Victoria and Albert Museum *bottom*.

Picture Research: Jackie Cookson